CHRISTMAS FAVORITES

Solos and Band Arrangements
Correlated with Essential Elements Band Method

ARRANGED BY
MICHAEL SWEENEY

Welcome to Essential Elements Christmas Favorites! There are two versions of each holiday selection in this versatile book:
1. The SOLO version (with lyrics) appears on the left-hand page.
2. The FULL BAND arrangement appears on the right-hand page.
Use the optional accompaniment tape when playing solos for friends and family. Your director may also use the accompaniment tape in band rehearsals and concerts.

ISBN 0-7935-1752-4

HAL•LEONARD® CORPORATION
7777 W. BLUEMOUND RD. P.O. BOX 13819 MILWAUKEE, WI 53213

JINGLE BELLS

Words and Music by J. PIERPONT
Arranged by MICHAEL SWEENEY

Solo

Introduction

5

Jin - gle Bells, Jin - gle Bells, Jin - gle all the way.

Oh what fun it is to ride in a one horse o - pen sleigh!

13

Jin - gle Bells, Jin - gle Bells, Jin - gle all the way.

Oh what fun it is to ride in a one horse o - pen sleigh!

21 **Interlude**

Oh what fun it is to ride in a one horse o - pen sleigh!

00862501

JINGLE BELLS

Words and Music by J. PIERPONT
Arranged by MICHAEL SWEENEY

Band Arrangement

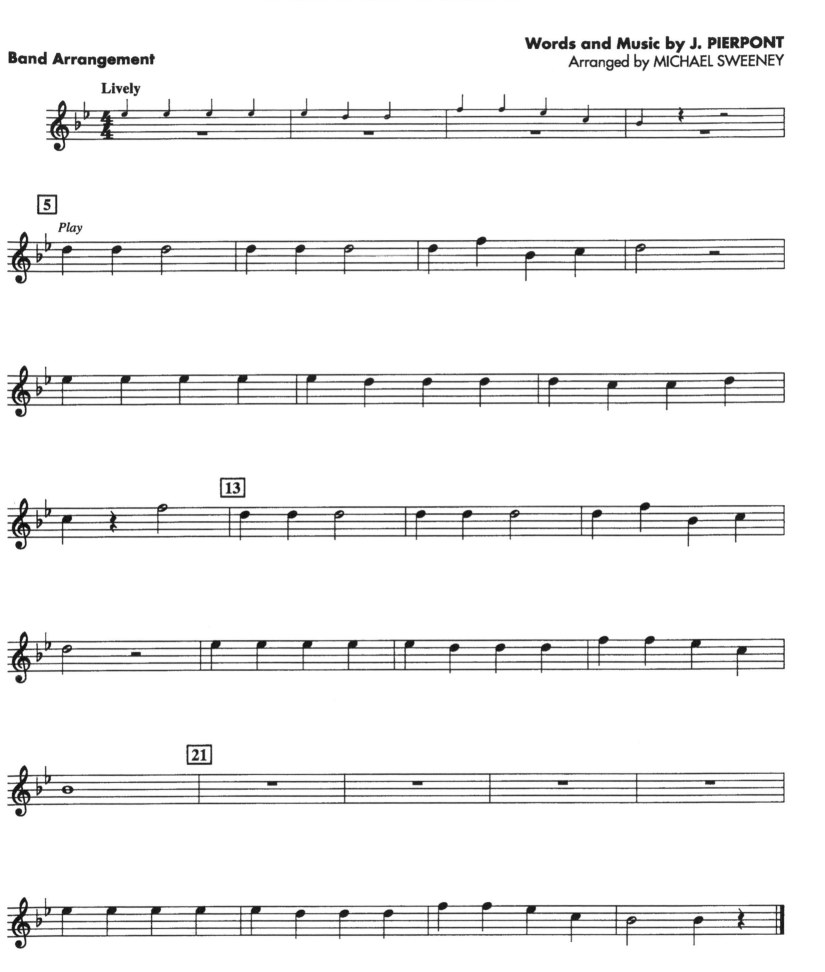

UP ON THE HOUSETOP

Arranged by MICHAEL SWEENEY

Solo

00862501

UP ON THE HOUSETOP

Band Arrangement

Arranged by MICHAEL SWEENEY

THE HANUKKAH SONG

Arranged by MICHAEL SWEENEY

Solo

THE HANUKKAH SONG

Band Arrangement

Arranged by MICHAEL SWEENEY

30862501

A HOLLY JOLLY CHRISTMAS

Music and Lyrics by JOHNNY MARKS
Arranged by MICHAEL SWEENEY

Solo

A Holly Jolly Christmas

Band Arrangement

Music and Lyrics by **JOHNNY MARKS**
Arranged by MICHAEL SWEENEY

WE WISH YOU A MERRY CHRISTMAS

Solo

Arranged by MICHAEL SWEENEY

We wish you a Mer-ry Christ-mas, We
all know that San-ta's com-ing, We

wish you a Mer-ry Christ-mas, We wish you a Mer-ry Christ-mas, and a
all know that San-ta's com-ing, We all know that San-ta's com-ing, and

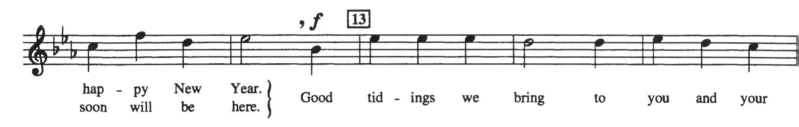

hap-py New Year.   Good tid-ings we bring to you and your
soon will be here.

kin, Good tid-ings for Christ-mas and a hap-py New

Year. We wish you a Mer-ry Christ-mas, We wish you a Mer-ry

Christ-mas, We wish you a Mer-ry Christ-mas, and a hap-py New

Year. Good tid-ings for Christ-mas and a hap-py New Year.

00862501

WE WISH YOU A MERRY CHRISTMAS

Band Arrangement

Arranged by MICHAEL SWEENEY

FROST, THE SNOWMAN

Words and Music by STEVE NELSON and JACK ROLLINS
Arranged by MICHAEL SWEENEY

Solo

FROSTY THE SNOW MAN

Words and Music by STEVE NELSON and JACK ROLLINS
Arranged by MICHAEL SWEENEY

Band Arrangement

ROCKIN' AROUND THE CHRISTMAS TREE

Music and Lyrics by JOHNNY MARKS
Arranged by MICHAEL SWEENEY

Solo

ROCKIN' AROUND THE CHRISTMAS TREE

Music and Lyrics by JOHNNY MARKS

Band Arrangement

Arranged by MICHAEL SWEENEY

00862501

JINGLE-BELL ROCK

Words and Music by JOE BEAL and JIM BOOTHE
Arranged by MICHAEL SWEENEY

Solo

JINGLE-BELL ROCK

**Words and Music by JOE BEAL
and JIM BOOTHE**
Arranged by MICHAEL SWEENEY

Band Arrangement

RUDOLPH THE RED-NOSED REINDEER

Music and Lyrics by JOHNNY MARKS
Arranged by MICHAEL SWEENEY

Solo

RUDOLPH THE RED-NOSED REINDEER

Music and Lyrics by JOHNNY MARKS
Arranged by MICHAEL SWEENEY

Band Arrangement

LET IT SNOW!
LET IT SNOW! LET IT SNOW!

Words by SAMMY CAHN
Music by JULE STYNE
Arranged by MICHAEL SWEENEY

Solo

LET IT SNOW! LET IT SNOW! LET IT SNOW!

Words by SAMMY CAHN
Music by JULE STYNE
Arranged by MICHAEL SWEENEY

Band Arrangement

00862501

THE CHRISTMAS SONG

Music and Lyric by MEL TORME and ROBERT WELLS

Arranged by MICHAEL SWEENEY

Solo

Chest-nuts roast-ing on an o-pen fire, Jack Frost nip-ping at your nose, Yule-tide carols be-ing sung by a choir and folks dressed up like Es-ki-mos. Ev-'ry-bod-y knows a tur-key and some mis-tle-toe help to make the sea-son bright. Ti-ny tots with their eyes all a-glow will find it hard to sleep to-night. They know that San-ta's on his way; He's load-ed lots of toys and good-ies on his sleigh. And ev-'ry moth-er's child __ is gon-na spy to see if reindeer real-ly know how to fly. And so I'm of-fer-ing this sim-ple phrase to kids from one to nine-ty-two. Al-tho' it's been said man-y times, man-y ways: "Mer-ry Christ-mas, Mer-ry Christ-mas, Mer-ry Christ-mas __ to you."

00862501

THE CHRISTMAS SONG

Music and Lyric by MEL TORME and ROBERT WELLS
Arranged by MICHAEL SWEENEY

Band Arrangement